MECHANICS

BY EMMA LESS

AMICUS READERS ● AMICUS INK

amicus
readers

Amicus Readers and Amicus Ink are imprints of Amicus
P.O. Box 1329, Mankato, MN 56002
www.amicuspublishing.us

Cataloging-in-Publication Data is on file with the Library of Congress.
ISBN 978-1-68151-300-3 (library binding)
ISBN 978-1-68152-282-1 (paperback)
ISBN 978-1-68151-362-1 (eBook)

Editor: Valerie Bodden
Designer: Patty Kelley

Photo Credits:
Cover: Goodluz/Adobe Stock Images
Inside: Adobe Stock: MNStudio 3. Dreamstime.com: Tyler Olson 4, Dmitry Kalinovsky 8, 16BR, Diego Vito Cervo 15, Uatp18 16T, Bizoon 16BL. Shutterstock: Lindasj22 6, Svariophoto 10, Michaeljung 12.

Printed in China.

HC 10 9 8 7 6 5 4 3 2 1
PB 10 9 8 7 6 5 4 3 2 1

Oh, no. Dina's family needs a mechanic. He will fix their car.

Mechanics work in a garage.

One mechanic opens
the car hood.
He looks
at the engine.

The car is on a lift.
There is room
to work under it.

The wrench helps
grab a bolt. Twist!
The bolt comes loose!

Fixing a car
is dirty work.
Time to clean up!

The work is done!
The car
is safe to drive!

SEEN AT A GARAGE

lift

tires

wrench